MEDITERRANEAN DIET COOKBOOK

50+ Dessert Recipes

How to Eat and Live Well with These recipes to Stay Healthy and Reach Your Ideal Weight

(2^ edition)

Antonio Fiorucci

Table of Contents

Introduction

The Mediterranean diet is a diet developed in the United States in the 1980s and inspired by Italy and Greece's eating habits in the 1960s. This diet's main aspects include proportionally high intake of olive oil, nuts and seeds, unprocessed cereals, fruits, veggies, moderate to high fish consumption, and regular drinking of dairy products (mostly as cheese and yogurt). Olive oil has been known as a potential health factor in reducing mortality from all causes and the risk of chronic diseases.

The Mediterranean diet has been proven to be an excellent way of maintaining health and living a long, healthy life. It is undoubtedly a great diet plan to follow. The Italian Mediterranean diet can also create long-term effects in keeping one's heart-healthy and body functioning at optimum levels. That is why the American Medical Association and the (AHA) American Heart Association suggest this diet.

Mediterranean Diet is a lifestyle more than a mere diet. It's safe to say the Mediterranean diet is both a brain-friendly and a body-friendly diet because it preserves and keeps them balanced in their respective ways. Therefore, as long as you follow this Mediterranean diet and continue to enrich your lifestyle with the balanced meal options it provides, you are assured of leading a safe and wonderful life without diseases hiding nearby.

Brief History of Italian Cuisine

The first traces of Italian cuisine date back to ancient times, when Sicily was among the Roman Empire's most important provinces. Then, when the Roman Empire fell, in AD 476, Sicily was occupied by the Ostrogoths for 300 years, unlike most of Italy's rest. During this time, some of the earliest cookbooks for cooking, Apicius, was written. Apicius and other cookbooks played a role in passing on to successive generations the cooking traditions of antiquity. Salvius was a chef who lived around 400 and a half centuries ago. His cooking was done in what was called the kitchen of gastronomy. It was a place where chefs of the Imperial Court gathered. Some recipes found in Apicius are very elaborate. Another essential cookbook from this period is De Re Coquinaria; Maestro Martino wrote this. This cookbook contains elements of Arab, Moorish, and Northern European cooking.

The first Italian cookbook written in 1472 is known as a book of the table's pleasures. This cookbook did not give measurements to the **directions** for the recipes. Instead, it included many different versions of **ingredients** and flavors.

In 1475, Fornaio was written by a person named Bartolomeo Sacchi, known as Platina. This book was the first cookbook written in the Italian language. It contained around 250 recipes that involved the measurement of the **ingredients**.

Platina described the different meals to be served. Platina included the proper foods to serve, such as the right **ingredients** to buy from a market and the foods that should be avoided. The recipes were very elaborate and complicated. In this book, there were numerous rules about food preparation, how many dishes should be ready for a meal, how many guests to serve, and how to serve and clean up after the meal.

Around 1570, the Book of Cooking by Bartolomeo Scappi was written. Plinio il Vecchio (Gaius Plinius Secundus) is the first cooking author to mention olive oil in his recipes. It helped to develop the beginning of the first cookbook by Bartol Omeo Scappi. He was an Italian monk and scientist from Padua, Italy. In 1570, he became the private cook for the powerful Medici family in Florence, Italy. He started to work and create recipes for them. His cookbook was written to help give the Medici family a reputation of being wealthy and sophisticated.

This cookbook mainly contained recipes for desserts, sweets, and different types of cocktails. A variety of meats and vegetables were used in these recipes, including many kinds of seafood. Many of the fruits in these recipes were imported from different countries such as Turkey and Sicily. There were a lot of **ingredients** and recipes that were imported from other countries as well. The book included around 400 recipes. He also had instructions on how to make different dishes.

Many of the recipes were based on different ones from around Europe. He made simple Italian recipes for more complicated dishes. For example, he used a chicken breast and then took fat pork belly and added it to the meat." Scappi also had a recipe for rabbit stuffed with bacon and chicken pigeons tied with leeks." It is an example of how he would change an already high dish and make it even higher. There is a difference between these high-class recipes and lower-class recipes. The high-class recipes were more complicated and more entertaining. The low-class recipes were less extravagant.

For the food, the dishes had only one main course. It was a sit-down dinner or an important meal. They had many different types of bread and desserts to choose from. The bread and bread products were made of many different grains and types of flour. The bread was the primary source of food in the lower classes.

Along with bread, the people had boiled greens and boiled meats. The greens were cooked with vinegar and butter-based sauce. The meats were boiled in water with salt. The meats were boiled and put into something to make it easier to eat. They had a different type of meat called frassetto, similar to beef, but it was more tender. Other meats were also consumed. The meat was slowly roasted in an oven called a spit. All classes liked the bread. People from every social class were able to buy and enjoy the bread.

The **ingredients** that the people used was essential. The vegetables included onions, leeks, escarole, cabbage, beans, Romano beans, carrots, lettuce, garlic, and legume. The basic types of cheese were mozzarella, Parmesan, ricotta, butter cheese from Tuscany, and sheep's cheese. Baked goods included butter cakes, puff pastry cakes, and cakes made of apricots, dates, and nuts. The wine included certain types made in Sicily. The drinks included mead, honeyed, and carob drinks, and the meats included beef, veal, mutton, pork, wild boar, goat, goose, chicken, duck, geese, and partridge.

The food wasn't the only thing of importance. The way that the food was served and the decor was important too. The hosts of these dinners and the guests had to dress up as well. The guests wore unique clothes; the women wore silk, velvet, and cotton velvets, and the men also wore silk and velvet. The tableware was usually made of gold, silver, and porcelain. They also used wood that was overlaid with the mother of pearl. It was used by the wealthier people who didn't need to decorate their tableware.

The food of the middle class was a little different from the upper class. The middle class had food with an emphasis on herbs, such as sage, rosemary, and mint. The middle class cooked plainer foods and mainly used grains. The foods that the middle class served were used to entertain guests and also for dinner. The dinner was the more formal meal of the day.

As Italy's food started to change and develop, so did the rooms and space used to serve the food. Initially, they would use the kitchen and the dining room in one area. There were no separate rooms for cooking and eating in Italy. After this style, the French style came around. This style had many rooms. The rooms were a big deal because they created more organization for the service of the food. The rooms were called the entrée, the cellar, the pantry, the scullery, the larder, the kitchen, the meat larder, the pastry room, and the servant's bedroom. The meat larder and the larder were the most important parts of the kitchen.

In the larder, the food was kept and cooked. In the meat, the larder was where the meat was kept cold. The room had a window so that the cold air could come through and keep the food cold. The larders are usually dark and low. The shape of the room is rectangular. The room is generally in the shape of a desk. The food is kept on a shelf that is built into the room. In a lot of larders, there is no electricity. It means that the food and food products can't be kept as cold. The larders are either fake or real. It is common for fake larders to be created in apartments.

The food served to the Italian people was very diverse, and it changed as many cultures influenced it. Some of these cultures were Chinese, early Indian, and Turkish. Each culture influenced the food and the way that the food was prepared. Also, as new cultures were introduced to Italy, the food changed with it.

Some of these cultures are known to us, and they, in turn, had their own cuisine. Other cultures stayed out of the public eye, and there is not much known about them that is useful. These cultures are all known, and there is more information available. The Turks were Italian allies in the sixteenth century, so there was a lot of trade between Turkey and Italy.

There are also Arab and Chinese influences that were not as well documented. Arab cuisine was developed in Italy as well.

In the 15th century, a new concept of food from this area was introduced. A strong Italian influence on cooking was created, and Justin Barrett wrote the book Cooking with Grease. In the 20th century, the Italian Mediterranean diet's essential elements were established, including a high intake of vegetables, fruit, and olive oil. However, the cuisine itself was not as refined as it is today. Before the mid-19th century, food often consisted of essential vegetable and meat stews and casseroles.

It is essential to know that the Italian Mediterranean diet now is a safe stronghold for us to hold onto and make it known to people to lead a healthy life. Nonetheless, its disappearance is a real danger and a threat to the good society we have long worked for and envisaged.

About the Mediterranean Diet

The Mediterranean diet is full of never-ending varieties of healthy, fresh, and delicious foods. However, there is more of an emphasis on certain types of foods, nothing is excluded. People who try a Mediterranean diet can enjoy the dishes they love while also learning to appreciate how good the freshest, healthiest foods can be.

Transitioning into the Mediterranean diet is mainly about bracing yourself for a new way of eating, adapting your attitude toward food into one of joyful expectation and appreciation of good meals and good company. It's like a mindset as anything else, so you'll want to make your environment unite so you can quickly adapt to the lifestyle in the Mediterranean way.

Benefits of the Mediterranean Diet

Boosts Your Brain Health: Preserve memory and prevent cognitive decline by following the Mediterranean diet that will limit processed foods, refined bread, and red meats. Have a glass of wine versus hard liquor.

Improves Poor Eyesight: Older individuals suffer from poor eyesight, but in many cases, the Mediterranean diet has provided notable improvement. An Australian Center for Eye Research discovered that the individuals who consumed a minimum of 100 ml (0.42 cup) of olive oil weekly were almost 50% less likely to develop macular degeneration versus those who ate less than one ml each week.

Helps to Reduce the Risk of Heart Disease: The New England Journal of Medicine provided evidence in 2013 from a randomized clinical trial. The trial was implemented in Spain, whereas individuals did not have cardiovascular disease at enrollment but were in the 'high risk' category. The incidence of major cardiovascular events was reduced by the Mediterranean diet that was supplemented with extra-virgin olive oil or nuts. In one study, men who consumed fish in this manner reduced the risk by 23% of death from heart disease.

The Risk of Alzheimer's disease is reduced: In 2018, the journal Neurology studied 70 brain scans of individuals who had no signs of dementia at the onset. They followed the eating patterns in a two-year study resulting in individuals who were on the Med diet had a lesser increase of the depots and reduced energy use - potentially signaling risk for Alzheimer's.

Helps Lessen the Risk of Some Types of Cancer: According to the results of a group study, the diet is associated with a lessened risk of stomach cancer (gastric adenocarcinoma).

Decreases Risks for Type 2 Diabetes: It can help stabilize blood sugar while protecting against type 2 diabetes with its low-carb elements. The Med diet maintains a richness in fiber, which will digest slowly while preventing variances in your blood sugar. It also can help you maintain a healthier weight, which is another trigger for diabetes.

Suggests Improvement for Those with Parkinson's disease: By consuming foods on the Mediterranean diet, you add high levels of antioxidants that can prevent your body from undergoing oxidative stress, which is a damaging process that will attack your cells. The menu plan can reduce your risk factors in half.

Mediterranean Diet Pyramid

The Mediterranean Diet Pyramid is a nutritional guide developed by the World Health Organization, Harvard School of Public Health, and Oldways Preservation Trust in 1993. It is a visual tool that summarizes the Mediterranean diet, suggested eating patterns, and guides how frequently specific mechanisms should be eaten. It allows you to break healthy eating habits and not overfill yourself with too many calories.

Olive oil, fruits, vegetables, whole grains, legumes, beans, nuts & seeds, spices & herbs: These foods form the Mediterranean pyramid base. If you did observe, you would notice that these are mostly from plant sources. You should try and include a few variations of these items into each meal you eat. Olive oil should be the primary fat in cooking your dishes and endeavor to replace any other butter or cooking oil you may have been using to cook.

Fish & seafood: These are essential staples of the Mediterranean diet that should be consumed often as a protein source. You would want to include these in your diet at least two times a week. Try new varieties of fish, either frozen or fresh. Also, incorporate seafood like mussels, crab, and shrimp into your diet. Canned tuna is also great to include on sandwiches or toss in a salad with fresh vegetables.

Cheese, yogurt, eggs & poultry: These **ingredients** should be consumed in more moderate amounts. Depending on the food, they should be used sparingly throughout the week. Keep in mind that if you are using eggs in baking or cooking, they will also be counted in your weekly limit. You would want to stick to more healthy cheese like Parmesan, ricotta, or feta that you can add a topping or garnish on your dishes.

Red meat & sweets: These items are going to be consumed less frequently. If you are going to eat them, you need to consume only small quantities, most preferably lean meat versions with less fat when possible. Most studies recommend a maximum of 12 to 16 ounces per month. To add more variety to your diet, you can still have red meat occasionally, but you would want to reduce how often you have it. It is essential to limit its intake because of all the health concerns of sugar and red meat. The Mediterranean diet improves cardiovascular health and reduces blood pressure, while red meat tends to be dangerous to your cardiovascular system. The Greece population ate very little red meat and instead had fish or seafood as their main protein source.

Water: The Mediterranean diet encourages you to stay hydrated at all times. It means drinking more water than your daily intake. The Institute of Medicine recommends a total of 9 cups each day for women and 13 cups for men. For pregnant or breastfeeding women, the number should be increased.

Wine: Moderate consumption of wine with meals is encouraged on the Mediterranean diet. Studies shown that moderate consumption of alcohol can reduce the risk of heart disease. That can mean about 1 glass per day for women. Men tend to have higher body mass so that they can consume 1 to 2 drinks. Please keep in mind what your doctor would recommend regarding wine consumption based on your health and family history.

The Mediterranean Food Pyramid

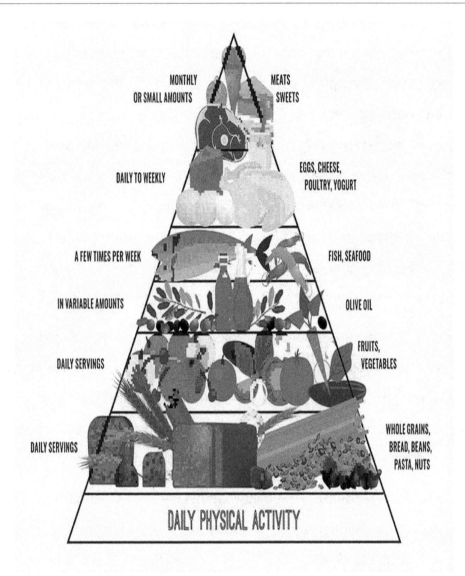

The Mediterranean Diet Pyramid is a visual tool that summarizes the Mediterranean Diet's suggested pattern of eating and gives a guide to how frequently specific tools should be eaten. This allows you to have a breakdown of healthy eating habits and not overfill yourself with too many calories.

How is the pyramid laid out? Let's go over each tier.

Olive oil, fruits, vegetables, whole grains, legumes, beans, nuts & seeds, spices & herbs: These are the types of food that form the base of the Mediterranean pyramid. You'll notice that these are mostly from plant sources. You should try and include a few variations of these items into each meal you eat. Olive oil should be the main fat you use in your cooking and your dishes, so replace any other butter or cooking oil you used to use. Generous uses of herbs and spices are also encouraged to season your food and add flavor as an alternative to salt. If you don't have access to fresh herbs, you can buy the dried version. Always be sure to read the nutrition labels to ensure there are no other **ingredients** mixed with the herbs. Fresh ginger and garlic are also great flavor enhancers for your meals. They can be easily stored in the freezer.

Fish & seafood: These are important staples of the Mediterranean diet that should be consumed often as a protein source. You want to try and include these in your diet at least two times a week. Try new varieties of fish, either frozen or fresh. Also incorporate seafood like mussels, crab, and shrimp into your diet. Canned tuna is also great to include on sandwiches or toss in a salad with fresh vegetables.

Cheese, yogurt, eggs & poultry: These **ingredients** should be consumed in more moderate amounts when on the Mediterranean diet. Depending on the food, they should be used sparingly throughout the week. Keep in mind that if you are using eggs in baking or cooking, those will also be counted in your weekly limit. You want to stick to more healthy cheese like Parmesan, ricotta, or feta that you can add as a topping or garnish on your dishes.

Red meat & sweets: These items are going to be consumed less frequently when on the Mediterranean diet. If you are eating them, you want to be sure it is only in small quantities and prefer lean meat versions with less fat. Most studies recommend a maximum of 12 to

18

16 ounces per month. You can still have red meat on occasion to add some variety to your diet, but you want to reduce how often you have it. That's because of all the health concerns that come with sugar and red meat. The Mediterranean diet is working to improve cardiovascular health and reduce blood pressure, while red meat tends to be dangerous in terms of cardiac health. The residents of Greece ate very little red meat and instead had fish or seafood as their main source of protein.

Water: The Mediterranean diet encourages you to be hydrated so that means drinking more than your daily intake of water. The Institute of Medicine recommends a total of 9 cups each day for women, and 13 cups for men. If a woman is pregnant or breastfeeding, that number should be increased.

Wine: Moderate consumption of wine with meals is encouraged on the Mediterranean diet. Studies have shown that moderate consumption of alcohol can reduce the risk of heart disease. That can mean about 1 glass per day for women. Men tend to have higher body mass so they can consume 1 to 2 glasses. Please keep in mind what your doctor would recommend regarding wine consumption based on your individual health and family history.

What To Eat: The Mediterranean Diet Food List

The Mediterranean diet is a very beneficial diet. That said, it is very hard for you to experience any of the benefits that you have just learned without following the diet to the latter. One way of doing that is by eating what the diet allows and avoiding what the diet prohibits you to eat. Let's get started

What you can eat

The foods you can eat while you are on a Mediterranean diet fall into two categories. There are those foods that you can eat regularly and there are those that you should only eat in moderation. Here is an extensive list of both categories.

Foods to eat regularly

Healthy fats like avocado oil, avocados, olives and extra virgin olive oil

Fruits like peaches, figs, melons, dates, bananas, strawberries, grapes, pears, oranges, and apples. Note that you can eat most fruits while on this diet

Vegetables like cucumbers, Brussels sprouts, artichoke, eggplant, carrots, cauliflower, onions, spinach, kale, broccoli and tomatoes. Those are just popular examples but basically all vegetables are allowed in the Mediterranean diet

Whole grains like pasta, whole wheat, whole grain bread, corn, buckwheat, barley, rye, brown rice and whole oats.

Nuts and seeds like pumpkin seeds, cashews, pistachios, walnuts, almonds and macadamia nuts

Herbs and spices; the best herbs and spices are mostly fresh and dried like mint, rosemary, cinnamon, basil and pepper.

Tubers like sweet potatoes, yams, turnips and potatoes.

Legumes like chickpeas, peanuts, pulses, lentils, peas and beans.

Fish and seafood, which are actually your primary source of protein. Good examples include shellfish like crab, mussels and oysters, shrimp, tuna, haddock and salmon.

Foods You Should Eat In Moderation

You should only eat the below foods less frequently when compared to the foods in the list above.

Red meat like bacon, ground beef and steak

Dairy products low in fat or fat free. Some of the popular examples include cheese, yogurt and low fat milk

Eggs, as they are good sources of proteins and are healthier when poached and boiled

Poultry like duck, turkey and chicken

Note that chicken are healthy when their skin is removed. This is because you reduce the cholesterol in the chicken.

Later on in the book, this list of foods that you are allowed to eat when on a Mediterranean diet will be expanded further where you will know what foods to take on a daily, weekly and monthly basis.

Food to Avoid

The below list contains a couple of foods that you need to avoid when on a Mediterranean diet completely. This is because they are unhealthy and when you eat them, you will be unable to experience the benefits of a Mediterranean diet. These foods include;

Processed meat- you should avoid processed meats like bacon, sausage and hot dogs because they are high in saturated fats, which are unhealthy.

Refined oils - stay away from unhealthy oils like cottonseed oil, vegetable oil and soybean oil.

Saturated or Trans-fats - good example of these fats include butter and margarine.

Highly processed foods – avoid all highly processed foods. By this, I mean all the foods that are packaged. This can be packaged crisp, nuts, wheat etc. Some of these foods are marked and labeled low fat but are actually quite high in sugar.

Refined grains - avoid refined grains like refined pasta, white bread, cereals, bagels etc

Added sugar- foods, which contain added sugar like sodas, chocolates, candy and ice cream should be completely avoided. If you have a sweet tooth, you can substitute products with added sugar with natural sweeteners.

Now that you know what to eat and what not to eat when on the Mediterranean diet you are now ready to learn how you can adopt the diet. The next chapter will show you how to do that.

Common Mistakes

When you start a new diet, you will make some mistakes or encounter situations in which you don't know what to do. Before you get on the Mediterranean diet plan, here is a heads up about common mistakes that people make. If you know about these mistakes, you can avoid them and achieve success more quickly.

- All or nothing

Your attitude towards the diet matters a lot. This is why you must make sure you are mentally prepared for the diet. It will be different from your ordinary lifestyle, which is why you need an abundance of information about it. To learn the benefits of this diet, you can ask the experts or people who have experienced it. You may experience mood or physical changes while adopting this lifestyle but there is nothing to worry about because it is all for your own benefit. When you see this diet as all or nothing you are looking at it from a short-term perspective and will end up abandoning it. Instead, be prepared to follow this diet strictly so that you will see a big difference.

- The same things

Don't eat the same things over and over again, every day. One of the most common mistakes people make is that they think that eating the same kind of vegetables all week long will help them lose weight. This is incorrect. You must have variety in your diet. The Mediterranean diet doesn't require that you consume only one ingredient all week long. It allows you to have multiple kinds of dishes throughout the week, but maintain portion control. You can eat chicken and eggs, but control your portions and eat according to the point system you have established for yourself. By the end of this book, you will be able to create a meal plan that will help you eat different kinds of food all week long. Don't eat the same things all the time because then you will be losing nutrients, which will eventually make you weak.

- Deprivation

Another mistake people make is thinking that deprivation is the only way to lose weight. The main point of this diet plan is to give you energy while helping you lose weight. Deprivation will only make you weaker. This diet plan won't work if you don't eat at all, so be sure to stick this point in your brain.

- Giving up

Don't give up in the middle of the Mediterranean diet because then it will have been of no use. If you see yourself losing weight and you think, 'Now I can have sweet things" … well, that's not the way to do it. If you have decided to follow it, do so. Stick to it no matter what. If you have cravings for chocolate, find a healthy alternative rather than giving up. This way, you will develop self-control and won't get into bad eating habits. Our bodies need time to adjust and stabilize in terms of the food we eat, which is why switching back and forth is never a good option.

- Not setting goals

One of the main mistakes people make is not setting goals when they start the diet. You must have a goal in terms of how much weight you want to lose and work accordingly. Some people may take six months to reach their goal, while some many take only months. It depends on your body type and the goal you set. If you like to go slow, that is your goal and you won't see an immediate difference. On the other hand, if you have a goal to lose five pounds in one month, you will be sticking strictly to the diet plan without missing a meal. When you don't have a plan, you will become distracted and be unable to reach your destination, no matter how hard you try.

- Following the wrong plan

Another common mistake is that you don't have enough knowledge about the plan you are following to lose weight. Maybe you are following the wrong plan, one that doesn't seem to work for you. If you're confused, don't make the decision by yourself to follow the Mediterranean plan; instead, consult an expert who can advise you on what to eat and do to adopt a healthy lifestyle. Many people follow their own style while mixing in elements of the Mediterranean diet, but if you try to modify the dishes, you won't achieve the optimal results. Make sure you follow the plan and prepare the correct recipes at home.

Eating Out On The Mediterranean Diet

It has been scientifically proven that the best and effective diets are mostly the ones that work with the body's natural process and internal environment to bring about the positive changes.

What Should you Have on Your Plate?

By now, you should already have a good idea of what to eat on the Mediterranean diet, but just to summarize:

• You should try to include fruits, seeds, nuts, vegetables, potatoes, bread, whole grain, herbs, fish, spices, seafood liberally and keep them in your platter.

• Eggs, yogurt, cheese, and poultry should be eaten in moderation.

• Beef, pork and other red meats should be eaten rarely or as minimally as possible.

• Completely avoid processed meat, sugar, sweetened beverages and refined grains from reaching your plate.

Your Shopping Guide

Aside from knowing how to start your diet, you should also know a little bit about how-to set-up your pantry.

What to go for

• All kinds of vegetables including tomatoes, kale, broccoli, spinach, cauliflower, Brussels sprouts, carrots, cucumbers, etc.

• All types of fruits such as orange, apple, banana, pears, grapes, dates, strawberries, figs, melons, peaches, etc.

- Nuts and seeds such as almonds, Macadamia, walnuts, cashews, sunflower seeds, pumpkin seeds, etc.

- Legumes such as beans, lentils, peas, pulses, chickpeas etc.

- Tubers such as yams, turnips, potatoes, sweet potatoes and so on

- Whole grains such as whole oats, rye, brown rice, corn, barley, buckwheat, whole wheat, whole grain pasta, and bread

- Fish and seafood such as sardines, salmon, tuna, shrimp, mackerel, oyster, crab, clams, mussels, etc.

- Poultry such as turkey, chicken, duck and more

- Eggs including duck, quail and chicken eggs

- Dairy such as cheese, Greek yogurt, etc.

- Herbs and spices such as mint, basil, garlic, rosemary, cinnamon, sage, pepper, etc.

- Healthy fats and oil such as extra virgin olive oil, avocado oil, olives, etc.

What to avoid

- Foods with added sugar such as soda, ice cream, candies, table sugar, etc.

- Refined grains such as white bread or pasta made with refined wheat

- Margarine and similar processed foods that contain Trans Fats

- Refined oil such as cottonseed oil, soybean oil, etc.

- Processed meat such as hot dogs, processed sausages and so on

- Highly processed food with labels such as "Low-Fat" or "Diet" or anything that is not natural

Oils to know about

The Mediterranean Diet emphasizes healthy oils. The following are some of the oils that you might want to consider.

Coconut Oil: This particular oil is semi-solid at room temperature and can be used for months without it turning rancid.

This particular oil also has a lot of health benefits! Since this oil is rich in a fatty acid known as Lauric Acid, it can help to improve cholesterol levels and kill various pathogens.

Extra-Virgin Olive Oil: Olive Oils are renowned worldwide for being one of the healthiest oils, and this is exactly why the Mediterranean Diet uses this oil as its key ingredient.

Some recent studies have shown that olive oil can even help to improve health biomarkers such as increasing the HDL cholesterol and lowering the amount of bad LDL cholesterol.

Avocado Oil: The composition of Avocado oil is very similar to olive oil and as such, it holds similar health benefits. It can be used for many purposes as an alternative for olive oil (Such as cooking).

Healthy salt alternatives

Asides from replacing healthy oils, the Mediterranean Diet will also ask you to opt for healthy salt alternatives as well. Below are some that you might want to consider.

Sunflower Seeds

Sunflower seeds are excellent and give a nutty and sweet flavor.

Fresh Squeezed Lemon

Lemon is believed to a be a nice hybrid between citron and bitter orange. These are packed with Vitamin C, which helps to neutralize damaging free radicals from the system.

Onion Powder

Onion powder is a dehydrated ground spice made from onion bulb, which is mostly used as a seasoning and is a fine salt alternative.

Black Pepper Powder

The black pepper powder is also a salt alternative that is native to India. Use it by grinding whole peppercorns!

Cinnamon

Cinnamon is very well-known as a savory spice, and two varieties are available: Ceylon and Chinese. Both of them sport a kind of sharp, warm and sweet flavor.

Flavored Vinegar

Fruit infused vinegar or flavored vinegar as we call it in our book are mixtures of vinegar that are combined with fruits in order to give a nice flavor. These are excellent **ingredients** to add a bit of flavor to meals without salt. Experimentation might be required to find the perfect fruit blend for you.

As for the process of making the vinegar:

- Wash your fruits and slice them well

- Place ½ a cup of your fruit in a mason jar

- Top them up with white wine vinegar (or balsamic vinegar)

- Allow them to sit for 2 weeks or so

- Strain and use as needed

Eating Out on the Mediterranean Diet

Initially, it might seem a little bit confusing, but eating out at a restaurant while on a Mediterranean Diet is actually pretty easy. Just follow the steps below:

- Try to ensure that you choose seafood or fish as the main dish of your meal

- When ordering, try to make a special request and ask the restaurant to fry their food using extra virgin olive oil

- Ask for only whole-grain based **ingredients** if possible

- If possible, try to read the menu of the restaurant before going there

- Try to have a simple snack before you go to the restaurant; this will help prevent you from overeating

Getting Started with the Mediterranean Diet and Meal Planning

The Mediterranean diet is a straightforward, easy to follow, and delicious diet, but you need a bit of preparation. Preparing for the Mediterranean diet is largely about preparing yourself for a new way of eating and adjusting your attitude toward food into one of joyful expectation and appreciation of good meals and good company.

Planning Your Mediterranean Diet

There are a few things to make your transition to the diet easier and effortless.

Ease your way into more healthful eating:

Before starting the diet, it can be helpful to spend a week or two cutting back on the least healthful foods that you are currently eating. You might start with fast food or eliminate cream-based sauces and soups. You can begin by cutting back on processed foods like frozen meals, boxed dinners, and chips. Some other things to start trimming might be sodas, coffee with a lot of sugar, and milk. You should lower butter, and cut out red meats such as lamb, beef, and pork.

Start thinking about what you'll be eating:

Just like planning for a vacation, you need to plan your diet. Go through the list of foods you need to eat on the Mediterranean diet and get recipe and meal ideas.

Gather what you'll need:

Everything in the Mediterranean diet is easily found at farmers' markets, grocery stores, and seafood shops. Find out where your local farmers' markets are and spend a leisurely morning checking out what is available. Talk to the farmers about what they harvest and when. Building relationships with those vendors can lead to getting special deals and the best selection. You can join the CSA (Community Supported Agriculture) farm nearby. CSA farms are small farms that sell subscription packages of whatever they're growing that season.

For a moderate seasonal or weekly fee, the farm will supply you with enough of that week's harvest to feed your whole family. Freshness is important when following the Mediterranean diet. Joining a CSA is a great way to enjoy the freshness and peak flavor that is so important to the Mediterranean diet. The same is true for your local seafood market and butcher shop. Find out who's selling the freshest, most healthful meats and seafood and buy from them. When you're ready to start, create a shopping list and get as many of your **ingredients** from your new sources as you can.

Plan your week:

Planning ahead is essential to success. The diet is heavily plant-based, and you need to load up on fresh fruits, vegetables, and herbs each week. By keeping your pantry stocked with whole grains like whole-wheat pasta, polenta, dried or canned beans and legumes, olive oil, and even some canned, vegetables and fish, you can be sure that you'll always have the **ingredients** for a healthy meal.

Adjust your portions:

The idea behind the Mediterranean diet is to make up the bulk of your diet with plant-based foods like fruits, vegetables, whole grains, beans, and nuts. Foods like cheese, meat, and sweets are allowed, but they are consumed only occasionally and in small portions. One way to ensure that you're eating enough plant-based foods while following the Mediterranean diet is to fill half your plate with vegetables and fruit, then fill one-quarter with whole grains, and the last quarter your plate with protein such as beans, fish, shellfish, or poultry. Once every week or two, enjoy a small serving of red meat, such as beef or lamb, or use meat as an accent to add flavor to plant-based stews, sauces, or other dishes. Here are some guidelines that will help you visualize appropriate portions for the Mediterranean diet:

- One ½ cup serving of grains or beans are about the size of the palm of your hand.
- 1 cup of vegetables is as big as a baseball.
- One medium piece of fruit is as big as a tennis ball.
- One 1-ounce serving of cheese is about the size of a pair of dice.
- One 3-ounce portion of meat (pork, lamb, fish, beef, or poultry) is roughly the size of a deck of cards.

34

Desserts

Butter Pie

Preparation Time: 10 minutes

Cooking Time: 15 minutes

Servings: 2

Ingredients:

- 3 whole eggs
- 6 tbsp of all-purpose flour
- 1 ½ cup of milk
- Salt to taste
- 4 tbsp of butter
- 1 cup of skim sour cream
- 1 tbsp of ground red pepper

Directions:

Preheat the oven to 300°. Line in some baking paper over a baking dish and then set it aside.

Mix well three eggs, all-purpose flour, 2 table spoons of butter, milk, and salt.

Spread the mixture on a baking dish and then bake it for about 15 minutes.

When done, remove from the oven and cool for a while. Chop into bite-sized pieces and place on a serving plate. Pour 1 cup of sour cream.

Melt the remaining 2 table spoons of butter over a medium temperature. Add 1 tablespoon of ground red pepper and stir-fry for several minutes. Drizzle some of this mixture over the pie and serve immediately.

Nutrition:

Calories 317

Fat 17g

Carbs 36g

Protein 24g

Homemade Spinach Pie

Preparation Time: 20 minutes

Cooking Time: 30 minutes

Servings: 5

Ingredients:

- lb. fresh spinach
- 0.5 lb. fresh dandelion leaves
- ¼ cup of Feta cheese, crumbled
- ½ cup of sour cream
- ½ cup of blue cheese, chopped
- 2 eggs
- 2 tbsp of butter, melted
- Salt to taste
- 1 pack of pie crust
- Vegetable oil

Directions:

Preheat the oven to 350 degrees. Use 1 table spoon of butter to grease the baking dish.

Add the ingredients in a large bowl and then mix well. Grease the pie crust with some oil.

Spread the spinach mixture over the pie crust and roll. Place in a baking dish and then bake for about 30-40 minutes

Remove from the heat and serve warm.

Nutrition:

Calories 230

Fat 9g

Carbs 29g

Protein 11g

Blueberries Bowls

Preparation Time: 10 minutes

Cooking Time: 0 minutes

Servings: 4

Ingredients:

- 1 teaspoon vanilla extract

- 2 cups blueberries

- 1 teaspoon coconut sugar

- 8 ounces Greek yogurt

Directions:

1. Mix strawberries with the vanilla and the other **ingredients**, toss and serve cold.

Nutrition:

343 calories

13.4g fat

5.5g protein

Rhubarb Strawberry Crunch

Preparation Time: 20 minutes

Cooking Time: 60 minutes

Servings: 18

Ingredients:

- 3 tbsps. all-purpose flour
- 3 c. fresh strawberries, sliced
- 3 c. rhubarb, cubed
- 1 ½ c. flour
- 1 c. packed brown sugar
- 1 c. butter
- 1 c. oatmeal

Directions:

Preheat the oven to 374°F

In a medium bowl mix rhubarb, 3 tbsps flour, white sugar, and strawberries. Set the mixture in a baking dish.

In another bowl mix 1 ½ cups of flour, brown sugar, butter, and oats until a crumbly texture is obtained. You may use a blender.

Combine mixtures and place on the baking pan

Bake for 45 minutes or until crispy and light brown.

Nutrition:

Calories 253

Fat 10.8g

Carbs 38.1g

Protein 2.3g

Banana Dessert with Chocolate Chips

Preparation Time: 20 minutes

Cooking Time: 30 minutes

Servings: 24

Ingredients:

- 2/3 c. white sugar
- ¾ c. butter
- 2/3 c. brown sugar
- 1 egg, beaten
- 1 tsp. vanilla extract
- 1 c. banana puree
- 1 ¾ c. flour
- 2 tsps. baking powder
- ½ tsp. salt
- 1 c. semi-sweet chocolate chips

Directions:

Preheat oven at 350°F

In a bowl, add the sugars and butter and beat until lightly colored

Add the egg and vanilla.

Add the banana puree and stir

In another bowl mix baking powder, flour, and salt. Add this mixture to the butter mixture

Stir in the chocolate chips

Prepare a baking pan and place the dough onto it

Bake for 20 minutes and let it cool for 5 minutes before slicing into equal squares

Nutrition:

Calories 174

Fat 8.2g

Carbs 25.2g

Protein 1.7g

Cranberry and Pistachio Biscotti

Preparation Time: 20 minutes

Cooking Time: 60 minutes

Servings: 4

Ingredients:

- ¼ c. light olive oil
- ¾ c. white sugar
- 2 tsps. vanilla extract
- ½ tsp. almond extract
- 2 eggs
- 1 ¾ c. all-purpose flour
- ¼ tsp. salt
- 1 tsp. baking powder
- ½ c. dried cranberries
- 1 ½ c. pistachio nuts

Directions:

Preheat the oven at 300 F/ 148 C

Combine olive oil and sugar in a bowl and mix well

Add eggs, almond and vanilla extracts, stir

Add baking powder, salt, and flour

Add cranberries and nuts, mix

Divide the dough in half — form two 12 x 2-inch logs on a parchment baking sheet.

Set in the oven and bake for 35 minutes or until the blocks are golden brown. Set from oven and allow to cool for about 10 minutes.

Set the oven to 275 F/ 135 C

Cut diagonal trunks into 3/4-inch-thick slices. Place on the sides on the baking sheet covered with parchment

Bake for about 8 - 10 minutes or until dry

You can serve it both hot and cold

Nutrition:

Calories 92

Fat 4.3g

Carbs 11.7g

Protein 2.1g

Minty Watermelon Salad

Preparation Time: 10 minutes

Cooking Time: None

Servings: 6-8

Ingredients:

- 1 medium watermelon
- 1 cup fresh blueberries
- 2 tablespoons fresh mint leaves
- 2 tablespoons lemon juice
- ⅓ cup honey

Directions:

Cut the watermelon into 1-inch cubes. Put them in a bowl.

Evenly distribute the blueberries over the watermelon.

Cchop the mint leaves and then put them into a separate bowl.

Add the lemon juice and honey to the mint and whisk together.

Drizzle the mint dressing over the watermelon and blueberries. Serve cold

Nutrition:

Calories 238

Fat 1g

Carbs 61g

Protein 4g

Mascarpone and Fig Crostini

Preparation Time: 10 minutes

Cooking Time: 10 minutes

Servings: 6-8

Ingredients:

- 1 long French baguette
- 4 tablespoons (½ stick) salted butter, melted
- 1 (8-ounce) tub mascarpone cheese
- 1 (12-ounce) jar fig jam or preserves

Directions:

Preheat the oven to 350°F.

Slice the bread into ¼-inch-thick slices.

Lay out the sliced bread on a single baking sheet and brush each slice with the melted butter.

Put the singleaking sheet in the oven and toast the bread for 5 to 7 minutes, just until golden brown.

Let the bread cool slightly. Spread it about a tea spoon or so of the mascarpone cheese on each piece of bread.

Top with a teaspoon or so of the jam. Serve immediately.

Nutrition:

Calories 445

Fat 24g

Carbs 48g

Protein 3g

Crunchy Sesame Cookies

Preparation Time: 10 minutes

Cooking Time: 15 minutes

Servings: 14-16

Ingredients:

- 1 cup sesame seeds, hulled
- 1 cup sugar
- 8 tablespoons (1 stick) salted butter, softened
- 2 large eggs
- 1¼ cups flour

Directions:

Preheat the oven to 350°F. Toast the sesame seeds on a baking sheet for 3 minutes. Set aside and let cool.

Using a mixer, cream together the sugar and butter.

Put the eggs one at a time until well-blended.

Add the flour and toasted sesame seeds and mix until well-blended.

Drop spoonfuls of cookie dough onto a baking sheet and form them into round balls, about 1-inch in diameter, similar to a walnut.

Put in the oven and bake for 5 to 7 minutes or until golden brown.

Let the cookies cool and enjoy.

Nutrition:

Calories 218

Fat 12g

Carbs 25g

Protein 4g

Almond Cookies

Preparation Time: 5 minutes

Cooking Time: 10 minutes

Servings: 4-6

Ingredients:

- ½ cup sugar
- 8 tablespoons (1 stick) room temperature salted butter
- 1 large egg
- 1½ cups all-purpose flour
- 1 cup ground almonds or almond flour

Directions:

Preheat the oven to 375°F.

Using a mixer, cream together the sugar and butter.

Add the egg and mix until combined.

Alternately add the flour and ground almonds, ½ cup at a time, while the mixer is on slow.

Once everything is combined, line a baking sheet with parchment paper. Drop a tablespoon of dough on the baking sheet, keeping the cookies at least 2 inches apart.

Put the single baking sheet in the oven and bake just until the cookies start to turn brown around the edges for about 5 to 7 minutes.

Nutrition:

Calories 604

Fat 36g

Carbs 63g

Protein 11g

Baklava and Honey

Preparation Time: 40 minutes

Cooking Time: 1 hour

Servings: 6-8

Ingredients:

- 2 cups chopped walnuts or pecans
- 1 teaspoon cinnamon
- 1 cup of melted unsalted butter
- 1 (16-ounce) package phyllo dough, thawed
- 1 (12-ounce) jar honey

Directions:

Preheat the oven to 350°F.

In a bowl, combine the chopped nuts and cinnamon.

Using a brush, butter the sides and bottom of a 9-by-13-inch inch baking dish.

Take off the phyllo dough from the package and cut it to the size of the baking dish using a sharp knife.

Put one sheet of phyllo dough on the bottom of the dish, brush with butter, and repeat until you have 8 layers.

Sprinkle ⅓ cup of the nut mixture over the phyllo layers. Top with a sheet of phyllo dough, butter that sheet, and repeat until you have 4 sheets of buttered phyllo dough.

Sprinkle ⅓ cup of the nut mixture for another layer of nuts. Repeat the layering of nuts and 4 sheets of buttered phyllo until all the nut mixture is gone. The last layer should be 8 buttered sheets of phyllo.

Before you bake, cut the baklava into desired shapes; traditionally this is diamonds, triangles, or squares.

Bake the baklava for about 1 hour just until the top layer is golden brown.

While the baklava is baking, heat the honey in a pan just until it is warm and easy to pour.

Once the baklava is done baking, directly pour the honey evenly over the baklava and let it absorb it, about 20 minutes. Serve warm or at room temperature.

Nutrition:

Calories 1235

Fat 89g

Carbs 109g

Protein 18g

Date and Nut Balls

Preparation Time: 10 minutes

Cooking Time: 10 minutes

Servings: 6-8

Ingredients:

- 1 cup walnuts or pistachios
- 1 cup unsweetened shredded coconut
- 14 medjool dates, pits removed
- 8 tablespoons (1 stick) butter, melted

Directions:

Preheat the oven to 350°F.

Put the nuts on a baking sheet. Toast the nuts for 5 minutes.

Put the shredded coconut on a clean baking sheet; toast just until it turns golden brown, about 3 to 5 minutes (coconut burns fast so keep an eye on it). Once done, remove it from the oven and put it in a shallow bowl.

Inside a food processor with a chopping blade, put the nuts until they have a medium chop. Put the chopped nuts into a medium bowl.

Add the dates and melted butter to the food processor and blend until the dates become a thick paste. Pour the chopped nuts into the food processor with the dates and pulse just until the mixture is combined, about 5 to 7 pulses.

Remove the mixture from the food processor and scrape it into a large bowl.

To make the balls, spoon 1 to 2 tablespoons of the date mixture into the palm of your hand and roll around between your hands until you form a ball. Put the ball on a clean, lined baking sheet. Repeat this until all of the mixture is formed into balls.

Roll each ball in the toasted coconut until the outside of the ball is coated, put the ball back on the baking sheet, and repeat.

Put all the balls into the fridge for 20 minutes before serving so that they firm up. You can also store any leftovers inside the fridge in an airtight container.

Nutrition:

Calories 489

Fat 35g

Carbs 48g

Protein 5g

Creamy Rice Pudding

Preparation Time: 5 minutes

Cooking Time: 45 minutes

Servings: 6

Ingredients:

- 1¼ cups long-grain rice
- 5 cups whole milk
- 1 cup sugar

- 1 tablespoon of rose water/orange blossom water
- 1 teaspoon cinnamon

Directions:

Rinse the rice under cold water for 30 seconds.

Add the rice, milk, and sugar in a large pot. Bring to a gentle boil while continually stirring.

Lessen the heat to low and then let simmer for 40 to 45 minutes, stirring every 3 to 4 minutes so that the rice does not stick to the bottom of the pot.

Add the rose water at the end and simmer for 5 minutes.

Divide the pudding into 6 bowls. Sprinkle the top with cinnamon. Let it cool for over an hour before serving. Store in the fridge.

Nutrition:

Calories 394

Fat 7g

Carbs 75g

Protein 9g

Ricotta-Lemon Cheesecake

Preparation Time: 5 minutes

Cooking Time: 1 hour

Servings: 8-10

Ingredients:

- 2 (8-ounce) packages full-fat cream cheese
- 1 (16-ounce) container full-fat ricotta cheese
- 1½ cups granulated sugar
- 1 tablespoon lemon zest
- 5 large eggs
- Nonstick cooking spray

Directions:

Preheat the oven to 350°F.

Blend together the cream cheese and ricotta cheese.

Blend in the sugar and lemon zest.

Blend in the eggs; drop in 1 egg at a time, blend for 10 seconds, and repeat.

Put a 9-inch springform pan with a parchment paper and nonstick spray.

Wrap the bottom of the pan with foil. Pour the cheesecake batter into the pan.

To make a water bath, get a baking or roasting pan larger than the cheesecake pan. Fill the roasting pan about ⅓ of the way up with warm water. Put the cheesecake pan into the water bath. Put the whole thing in the oven and let the cheesecake bake for 1 hour.

After baking is complete, remove the cheesecake pan from the water bath and remove the foil. Let the cheese cake cool for 1 hour on the countertop. Then put it in the fridge to cool for at least 3 hours before serving.

Nutrition:

Calories 489

Fat 31g

Carbs 42g

Protein 15g

Crockpot Keto Chocolate Cake

Preparation Time: 20 minutes

Cooking Time: 3 hours

Servings: 12

Ingredients:

- ¾ c. stevia sweetener
- 1 ½ c. almond flour
- ¼ tsp. baking powder
- ¼ c. protein powder, chocolate, or vanilla flavor
- 2/3 c. unsweetened cocoa powder
- ¼ tsp. salt
- ½ c. unsalted butter, melted
- 4 large eggs
- ¾ c. heavy cream
- 1 tsp. vanilla extract

Directions:

Grease the ceramic insert of the Crockpot.

In a bowl, mix the sweetener, almond flour, protein powder, cocoa powder, salt, and baking powder.

Add the butter, eggs, cream, and vanilla extract.

Pour the batter in the Crockpot and cook on low for 3 hours.

Allow to cool before slicing.

Nutrition:

Calories: 253

Carbohydrates: 5.1g

Protein: 17.3g

Fat: 29.5g

Keto Crockpot Chocolate Lava Cake

Preparation Time: 30 minutes

Cooking Time: 3 hours

Servings: 12

Ingredients:

- 1 ½ c. stevia sweetener, divided
- ½ c. almond flour
- 5 tbsps. unsweetened cocoa powder
- ½ tsp. salt
- 1 tsp. baking powder
- 3 whole eggs
- 3 egg yolks
- ½ c. butter, melted
- 1 tsp. vanilla extract
- 2 c. hot water

- 4 ounces sugar-free chocolate chips

Directions:

Grease the inside of the Crockpot.

In a bowl, mix the stevia sweetener, almond flour, cocoa powder, salt, and baking powder.

In another bowl, mix the eggs, egg yolks, butter, and vanilla extract. Pour in the hot water.

Pour the wet **ingredients** to the dry **ingredients** and fold to create a batter.

Add the chocolate chips last

Pour into the greased Crockpot and cook on low for 3 hours.

Allow to cool before serving.

Nutrition:

Calories: 157

Carbohydrates: 5.5g

Protein: 10.6g

Fat: 13g

Lemon Crockpot Cake

Preparation Time: 15 minutes

Cooking Time: 3 hours

Servings: 8

Ingredients:

- ½ c. coconut flour
- 1 ½ c. almond flour
- 3 tbsps. stevia sweetener
- 2 tsps. baking powder
- ½ tsp. xanthan gum
- ½ c. whipping cream
- ½ c. butter, melted
- 1 tbsp. juice, freshly squeezed
- Zest from one large lemon
- 2 eggs

Directions:

Grease the inside of the Crockpot with a butter or cooking spray.

Mix together coconut flour, almond flour, stevia, baking powder, and xanthan gum in a bowl.

In another bowl, combine the whipping cream, butter, lemon juice, lemon zest, and eggs. Mix until well combined.

Pour the wet **ingredients** to the dry **ingredients** gradually and fold to create a smooth batter.

Spread the batter in the Crockpot and cook on low for 3 hours

Nutrition:

Calories: 350

Carbohydrates: 11.1g

Protein: 17.6g

Fat: 32.6g

Lemon and Watermelon Granita

Preparation Time: 10 minutes + 3 hours to freeze

Cooking Time: None

Servings: 4

Ingredients:

- 4 cups watermelon cubes
- ¼ cup honey
- ¼ cup freshly squeezed lemon juice

Directions:

In a blender, combine the watermelon, honey, and lemon juice. Purée all the **ingredients**, then pour into a 9-by-9-by-2-inch baking pan and place in the freezer.

Every 30 to 60 minutes, run a fork across the frozen surface to fluff and create ice flakes. Freeze for about 3 hours total and serve.

Nutrition:

Calories: 153

Carbohydrates: 39g

Protein: 2g

Fat: 1g

Baked Apples with Walnuts and Spices

Preparation Time: 10 minutes

Cooking Time: 45 minutes

Servings: 4

Ingredients:

- 4 apples
- ¼ cup chopped walnuts
- 2 tablespoons honey
- 1 teaspoon ground cinnamon
- ¼ teaspoon ground nutmeg

- ¼ teaspoon ground ginger
- Pinch sea salt

Directions:

Preheat the oven to 375°F.

Cut the tops off the apples and then use a metal spoon or a paring knife to remove the cores, leaving the bottoms of the apples intact. Place the apples cut-side up in a 9-by-9-inch baking pan.

Stir together the walnuts, honey, cinnamon, nutmeg, ginger, and sea salt. Put the mixture into the centers of the apples. Bake the apples for about 45 minutes until browned, soft, and fragrant. Serve warm.

Nutrition:

Calories: 199

Carbohydrates: 41g

Protein: 5g

Fat: 5g

Red Wine Poached Pears

Preparation Time: 10 minutes

Cooking Time: 45 minutes + 3 hours to chill

Servings: 4

Ingredients:

- 2 cups dry red wine
- ¼ cup honey
- Zest of ½ orange
- 2 cinnamon sticks
- 1 (1-inch) piece fresh ginger
- 4 pears, bottom inch sliced off so the pear is flat

Directions:

In a pot on medium-high heat, stir together the wine, honey, orange zest, cinnamon, and ginger. Bring to a boil, stirring occasionally. Lessen the heat to medium-low and then simmer for 5 minutes to let the flavors blend.

Add the pears to the pot. Cover and simmer for 20 minutes until the pears are tender, turning every 3 to 4 minutes to ensure even color and contact with the liquid. Refrigerate the pears in the liquid for 3 hours to allow for more flavor absorption.

Bring the pears and liquid to room temperature. Place the pears on individual dishes and return the poaching liquid to the stove top over medium-high heat. Simmer for 15 minutes until the liquid is syrupy. Serve the pears with the liquid drizzled over the top.

Nutrition:

Calories: 283

Carbohydrates: 53g

Protein: 1g

Fat: 1g

Vanilla Pudding with Strawberries

Preparation Time: 10 minutes

Cooking Time: 10 minutes + chilling time

Servings: 4

Ingredients:

- 2¼ cups skim milk, divided
- 1 egg, beaten
- ½ cup sugar
- 1 teaspoon vanilla extract

- Pinch sea salt
- 3 tablespoons cornstarch
- 2 cups sliced strawberries

Directions:

In a small bowl, whisk 2 cups of milk with the egg, sugar, vanilla, and sea salt. Transfer the mixture to a medium pot, place it over medium heat, and slowly bring to a boil, whisking constantly.

Whisk the cornstarch with the ¼ cup of milk. In a thin stream, whisk this slurry into the boiling mixture in the pot. Cook until it thickens, stirring constantly. Boil for 1 minute more, stirring constantly.

Spoon the pudding into 4 dishes and refrigerate to chill. Serve topped with the sliced strawberries.

Nutrition:

Calories: 209

Carbohydrates: 43g

Protein: 6g

Fat: 1g

Mixed Berry Frozen Yogurt Bar

Preparation Time: 10 minutes

Cooking Time: None

Servings: 8

Ingredients:

- 8 cups low-fat vanilla frozen yogurt (or flavor of choice)
- 1 cup sliced fresh strawberries
- 1 cup fresh blueberries
- 1 cup fresh blackberries
- 1 cup fresh raspberries
- ½ cup chopped walnuts

Directions:

Apportion the yogurt among 8 dessert bowls. Serve the toppings family style, and let your guests choose their toppings and spoon them over the yogurt.

Nutrition:

Calories: 81

Carbohydrates: 9g

Protein: 3g

Fat:

Vanilla Cream

Preparation Time: 2 hours

Cooking Time: 10 minutes

Servings: 4

Ingredients:

- 1 cup almond milk

- 1 cup coconut cream

- 2 cups coconut sugar

- 2 tablespoons cinnamon powder

- 1 teaspoon vanilla extract

Directions:

1. Heat up a pan with the almond milk over medium heat, add the rest of the **ingredients**, whisk, and cook for 10 minutes more.

2. Divide the mix into bowls, cool down and keep in the fridge for 2 hours before serving.

Nutrition:

254 calories

7.5g fat

9.5g protein

Brownies

Preparation Time: 10 minutes

Cooking Time: 25 minutes

Servings: 8

Ingredients:

- 1 cup pecans, chopped

- 3 tablespoons coconut sugar

- 2 tablespoons cocoa powder

- 3 eggs, whisked

- ¼ cup avocado oil

- ½ teaspoon baking powder

- 2 teaspoons vanilla extract

- Cooking spray

Directions:

1. In your food processor, combine the pecans with the coconut sugar and the other ingredients except the cooking spray and pulse well.

2. Grease a square pan with cooking spray, add the brownies mix, spread, introduce in the oven, bake at 350 degrees F for 25 minutes, leave aside to cool down, slice and serve.

Nutrition:

370 calories

14.3g fat

5.6g protein

Strawberries Coconut Cake

Preparation Time: 10 minutes

Cooking Time: 25 minutes

Servings: 6

Ingredients:

- 2 cups almond flour
- 1 cup strawberries, chopped
- ½ teaspoon baking soda
- ½ cup coconut sugar
- ¾ cup coconut milk
- ¼ cup avocado oil
- 2 eggs, whisked
- 1 teaspoon vanilla extract
- Cooking spray

Directions:

1. In a bowl, combine the flour with the strawberries and the other ingredients except the cooking spray and whisk well.
2. Grease a cake pan with cooking spray, pour the cake mix, spread, bake in the oven at 350 degrees F for 25 minutes, cool down, slice and serve.

Nutrition:

465 calories

22g fat

13.4g protein

Cocoa Almond Pudding

Preparation Time: 10 minutes

Cooking Time: 10 minutes

Servings: 4

Ingredients:

- 2 tablespoons coconut sugar

- 3 tablespoons coconut flour

- 2 tablespoons cocoa powder

- 2 cups almond milk

- 2 eggs, whisked

- ½ teaspoon vanilla extract

Directions:

1. Fill milk in a pan, add the cocoa and the other **ingredients**, whisk, simmer over medium heat for 10 minutes, pour into small cups and serve cold.

Nutrition:

385 calories

31.7g fat

7.3g protein

Nutmeg Cream

Preparation Time: 10 minutes

Cooking Time: 0 minutes

Servings: 6

Ingredients:

- 3 cups almond milk

- 1 teaspoon nutmeg, ground

- 2 teaspoons vanilla extract

- 4 teaspoons coconut sugar

- 1 cup walnuts, chopped

Directions:

1.   In a bowl, combine milk with the nutmeg and the other **ingredients**, whisk well, divide into small cups and serve cold.

Nutrition:

243 calories

12.4g fat

9.7g protein

Vanilla Avocado Cream

Preparation Time: 70 minutes

Cooking Time: 0 minutes

Servings: 4

Ingredients:

- 2 cups coconut cream

- 2 avocados, peeled, pitted and mashed

- 2 tablespoons coconut sugar

- 1 teaspoon vanilla extract

Directions:

1.   Blend cream with the avocados and the other **ingredients**, pulse well, divide into cups and keep in the fridge for 1 hour before serving.

Nutrition:

532 calories

48.2g fat

5.2g protein

Raspberries Cream Cheese Bowls

Preparation Time: 10 minutes

Cooking Time: 25 minutes

Servings: 4

Ingredients:

- 2 tablespoons almond flour

- 1 cup coconut cream

- 3 cups raspberries

- 1 cup coconut sugar

- 8 ounces cream cheese

Directions:

1. In a bowl, the flour with the cream and the other **ingredients**, whisk, transfer to a round pan, cook at 360 degrees F for 25 minutes, divide into bowls and serve.

Nutrition:

429 calories

36.3g fat

7.8g protein

Mediterranean Watermelon Salad

Preparation time: 4 minutes

Cooking time: 0 minutes

Servings: 4

Ingredients:

- 1 cup watermelon, peeled and cubed

- 2 apples, cored and cubed

- 1 tablespoon coconut cream

- 2 bananas, cut into chunks

Directions:

1.   Incorporate watermelon with the apples and the other **ingredients**, toss and serve.

Nutrition:

131 calories

1.3g fat

1.3g protein

Coconut Apples

Preparation Time: 10 minutes

Cooking Time: 10 minutes

Servings: 4

Ingredients:

- 2 teaspoons lime juice

- ½ cup coconut cream

- ½ cup coconut, shredded

- 4 apples, cored and cubed

- 4 tablespoons coconut sugar

Directions:

1. Incorporate apples with the lime juice and the other **ingredients**, stir, bring to a simmer over medium heat and cook for 10 minutes.

2. Divide into bowls and serve cold.

Nutrition:

320 calories

7.8g fat

4.7g protein

Orange Compote

Preparation Time: 10 minutes

Cooking Time: 15 minutes

Servings: 4

Ingredients:

- 5 tablespoons coconut sugar

- 2 cups orange juice

- 4 oranges, peeled and cut into segments

Directions:

1.   In a pot, combine oranges with the sugar and the orange juice, toss, bring to a boil over medium heat, cook for 15 minutes, divide into bowls and serve cold.

Nutrition:

220 calories

5.2g fat

5.6g protein

Pears Stew

Preparation Time: 10 minutes

Cooking Time: 15 minutes

Servings: 4

Ingredients:

- 2 cups pears, cored and cut into wedges
- 2 cups water
- 2 tablespoons coconut sugar
- 2 tablespoons lemon juice

Directions:

1. In a pot, combine the pears with the water and the other **ingredients**, toss, cook over medium heat for 15 minutes, divide into bowls and serve.

Nutrition:

260 calories

6.2g fat

6g protein

Lemon Watermelon Mix

Preparation Time: 10 minutes

Cooking Time: 10 minutes

Servings: 4

Ingredients:

- 2 cups watermelon

- 4 tablespoons coconut sugar

- 2 teaspoons vanilla extract

- 2 teaspoons lemon juice

Directions:

1. In a small pan, combine the watermelon with the sugar and the other **ingredients**, toss, heat up over medium heat, cook for about 10 minutes, divide into bowls and serve cold.

Nutrition:

140 calories

4g fat

5g protein

Rhubarb Cream

Preparation Time: 10 minutes

Cooking Time: 14 minutes

Servings: 4

Ingredients:

- 1/3 cup cream cheese

- ½ cup coconut cream

- 2-pound rhubarb, roughly chopped

- 3 tablespoons coconut sugar

Directions:

1. Blend cream cheese with the cream and the other **ingredients** well.

2. Divide into small cups, introduce in the oven and bake at 350 degrees F for 14 minutes.

3. Serve cold.

Nutrition:

360 calories

14.3g fat

5.2g protein

Mango Bowls

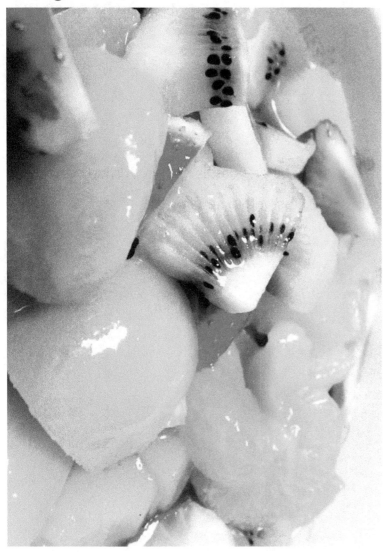

Preparation Time: 10 minutes

Cooking Time: 0 minutes

Servings: 4

Ingredients:

- 3 cups mango, peeled and cubed

- 1 teaspoon chia seeds

- 1 cup coconut cream

- 1 teaspoon vanilla extract

- 1 tablespoon mint, chopped

Directions:

1. Mix mango with the cream and the other **ingredients**, toss, divide into smaller bowls and keep in the fridge for 10 minutes before serving.

Nutrition:

238 calories

16.6g fat

3.3g protein

Chocolate Ganache

Preparation time: 10 minutes

Cooking Time: 16 minutes

Servings: 16

Ingredients

- 9 ounces bittersweet chocolate, chopped

- 1 cup heavy cream

- 1 tablespoon dark rum (optional)

Direction

1. Situate chocolate in a medium bowl. Cook cream in a small saucepan over medium heat.

2. Bring to a boil. When the cream has reached a boiling point, pour the chopped chocolate over it and beat until smooth. Stir the rum if desired.

3. Allow the ganache to cool slightly before you pour it on a cake. Begin in the middle of the cake and work outside. For a fluffy icing or chocolate filling, let it cool until thick and beat with a whisk until light and fluffy.

Nutrition:

142 calories

10.8g fat

1.4g protein

Chocolate Covered Strawberries

Preparation Time: 15 minutes

Cooking Time: 0 minute

Servings: 24

Ingredients

- 16 ounces milk chocolate chips

- 2 tablespoons shortening

- 1-pound fresh strawberries with leaves

Direction

1. In a bain-marie, melt chocolate and shortening, occasionally stirring until smooth. Pierce the tops of the strawberries with toothpicks and immerse them in the chocolate mixture.

2. Turn the strawberries and put the toothpick in Styrofoam so that the chocolate cools.

Nutrition:

115 calories

7.3g fat

1.4g protein

Strawberry Angel Food Dessert

Preparation Time: 15 minutes

Cooking Time: 0 minutes

Servings: 18

Ingredients

- 1 angel cake (10 inches)

- 2 packages of softened cream cheese

- 1 cup of white sugar

- 1 container (8 oz) of frozen fluff, thawed

- 1 liter of fresh strawberries, sliced

- 1 jar of strawberry icing

Direction

1. Crumble the cake in a 9 x 13-inch dish.

2. Beat the cream cheese and sugar in a medium bowl until the mixture is light and fluffy. Stir in the whipped topping. Crush the cake with your hands, and spread the cream cheese mixture over the cake.

3. Combine the strawberries and the frosting in a bowl until the strawberries are well covered. Spread over the layer of cream cheese. Cool until ready to serve.

Nutrition:

261 calories

11g fat

3.2g protein

Fruit Pizza

Preparation Time: 30 minutes

Cooking Time: 0 minute

Servings: 8

Ingredients

- 1 (18-oz) package sugar cookie dough

- 1 (8-oz) package cream cheese, softened

- 1 (8-oz) frozen filling, defrosted

- 2 cups of freshly cut strawberries

- 1/2 cup of white sugar

- 1 pinch of salt

- 1 tablespoon corn flour

- 2 tablespoons lemon juice

- 1/2 cup orange juice

- 1/4 cup water

- 1/2 teaspoon orange zest

Direction

1. Ready oven to 175 ° C Slice the cookie dough then place it on a greased pizza pan. Press the dough flat into the mold. Bake for 10 to 12 minutes. Let cool.

2. Soften the cream cheese in a large bowl and then stir in the whipped topping. Spread over the cooled crust.

3. Start with strawberries cut in half. Situate in a circle around the outer edge. Continue with the fruit of your choice by going to the center. If you use bananas, immerse them in lemon juice. Then make a sauce with a spoon on the fruit.

4. Combine sugar, salt, corn flour, orange juice, lemon juice, and water in a pan. Boil and stir over medium heat. Boil for 1 or 2 minutes until thick. Remove from heat and add the grated orange zest. Place on the fruit.

5. Allow to cool for two hours, cut into quarters, and serve.

Nutrition

535 calories

30g fat

5.5g protein

Bananas Foster

Preparation Time: 5 minutes

Cooking Time: 6 minutes

Servings: 4

Ingredients

- 2/3 cup dark brown sugar
- 1/4 cup butter
- 3 1/2 tablespoons rum
- 1 1/2 teaspoons vanilla extract
- 1/2 teaspoon of ground cinnamon
- 3 bananas, peeled and cut lengthwise and broad
- 1/4 cup coarsely chopped nuts
- vanilla ice cream

Direction

1. Melt the butter in a deep-frying pan over medium heat. Stir in sugar, rum, vanilla, and cinnamon.
2. When the mixture starts to bubble, place the bananas and nuts in the pan. Bake until the bananas are hot, 1 to 2 minutes. Serve immediately with vanilla ice cream.

Nutrition:

534 calories

23.8g fat

4.6g protein

Cranberry Orange Cookies

Preparation Time: 20 minutes

Cooking Time: 16 minutes

Servings: 24

Ingredients

- 1 cup of soft butter

- 1 cup of white sugar

- 1/2 cup brown sugar

- 1 egg

- 1 teaspoon grated orange peel

- 2 tablespoons orange juice

- 2 1/2 cups flour

- 1/2 teaspoon baking powder

- 1/2 teaspoon salt

- 2 cups chopped cranberries

- 1/2 cup chopped walnuts (optional)

Icing:

- 1/2 teaspoon grated orange peel

- 3 tablespoons orange juice

- 1 ½ cup confectioner's sugar

Direction

1. Preheat the oven to 190 ° C.

2. Blend butter, white sugar, and brown sugar. Beat the egg until everything is well mixed. Mix 1 teaspoon of orange zest and 2 tablespoons of orange juice. Mix the flour, baking powder, and salt; stir in the orange mixture.

3. Mix the cranberries and, if used, the nuts until well distributed. Place the dough with a spoon on ungreased baking trays.

4. Bake in the preheated oven for 12 to 14 minutes. Cool on racks.

5. In a small bowl, mix icing **ingredients**. Spread over cooled cookies.

Nutrition:

110 calories

4.8g fat

1.1 g protein

Key Lime Pie

Preparation time: 15 minutes

Cooking Time: 8 minutes

Servings: 8

Ingredients

- 1 (9-inch) prepared graham cracker crust
- 3 cups of sweetened condensed milk
- 1/2 cup sour cream
- 3/4 cup lime juice
- 1 tablespoon grated lime zest

Direction

1. Prepare oven to 175 ° C

2. Combine the condensed milk, sour cream, lime juice, and lime zest in a medium bowl. Mix well and pour into the graham cracker crust.

3. Bake in the preheated oven for 5 to 8 minutes

4. Cool the cake well before serving. Decorate with lime slices and whipped cream if desired.

Nutrition:

553 calories

20.5g fat

10.9g protein

Rhubarb Strawberry Crunch

Preparation time: 15 minutes

Cooking Time: 45 minutes

Servings: 18

Ingredients

- 1 cup of white sugar
- 3 tablespoons all-purpose flour
- 3 cups of fresh strawberries, sliced
- 3 cups of rhubarb, cut into cubes
- 1 1/2 cup flour
- 1 cup packed brown sugar
- 1 cup butter
- 1 cup oatmeal

Direction

1. Preheat the oven to 190 ° C.
2. Combine white sugar, 3 tablespoons flour, strawberries and rhubarb in a large bowl. Place the mixture in a 9 x 13-inch baking dish.
3. Mix 1 1/2 cups of flour, brown sugar, butter, and oats until a crumbly texture is obtained. You may want to use a blender for this. Crumble the mixture of rhubarb and strawberry.
4. Bake for 45 minutes.

Nutrition:

253 calories

10.8g fat

2.3g protein

Chocolate Chip Banana Dessert

Preparation Time: 20 minutes

Cooking Time: 20 minutes

Servings: 24

Ingredients

- 2/3 cup white sugar
- 3/4 cup butter
- 2/3 cup brown sugar
- 1 egg, beaten slightly
- 1 teaspoon vanilla extract
- 1 cup of banana puree
- 1 3/4 cup flour
- 2 teaspoons baking powder
- 1/2 teaspoon of salt
- 1 cup of semi-sweet chocolate chips

Direction:

1. Ready the oven to 175 ° C Grease and bake a 10 x 15-inch baking pan.

2. Beat the butter, white sugar, and brown sugar in a large bowl until light. Beat the egg and vanilla. Fold in the banana puree: mix baking powder, flour, and salt in another bowl. Mix flour mixture into the butter mixture. Stir in the chocolate chips. Spread in pan.

3. Bake for 20 minutes. Cool before cutting into squares.

Nutrition:

174 calories

8.2g fat

1.7g protein

Apple Pie Filling

Preparation time: 20 minutes

Cooking Time: 12 minutes

Servings: 40

Ingredients

- 18 cups chopped apples
- 3 tablespoons lemon juice
- 10 cups of water
- 4 1/2 cups of white sugar
- 1 cup corn flour
- 2 teaspoons of ground cinnamon
- 1 teaspoon of salt
- 1/4 teaspoon ground nutmeg

Direction

1. Mix apples with lemon juice in a large bowl and set aside. Pour the water in a Dutch oven over medium heat. Combine sugar, corn flour, cinnamon, salt, and nutmeg in a bowl. Add to water, mix well, and bring to a boil. Cook for 2 minutes with continuous stirring.
2. Boil apples again. Reduce the heat, cover, and simmer for 8 minutes. Allow cooling for 30 minutes.
3. Pour into five freezer containers and leave 1/2 inch of free space. Cool to room temperature.
4. Seal and freeze

Nutrition:

129 calories

0.1g fat

0.2g protein

Ice Cream Sandwich Dessert

Preparation Time: 20 minutes

Cooking Time: 0 minute

Servings: 12

Ingredients

- 22 ice cream sandwiches

- Frozen whipped topping in 16 oz container, thawed

- 1 jar (12 oz) Caramel ice cream

- 1 1/2 cups of salted peanuts

Direction

1. Cut a sandwich with ice in two. Place a whole sandwich and a half sandwich on a short side of a 9 x 13-inch baking dish. Repeat this until the bottom is covered, alternate the full sandwich, and the half sandwich.

2. Spread half of the whipped topping. Pour the caramel over it. Sprinkle with half the peanuts. Do layers with the rest of the ice cream sandwiches, whipped cream, and peanuts.

3. Cover and freeze for up to 2 months. Remove from the freezer 20 minutes before serving. Cut into squares.

Nutrition:

559 calories

28.8g fat

10g protein

Cranberry and Pistachio Biscotti

Preparation time: 15 minutes

Cooking Time: 35 minutes

Servings: 36

Ingredients

- 1/4 cup light olive oil
- 3/4 cup white sugar
- 2 teaspoons vanilla extract
- 1/2 teaspoon almond extract
- 2 eggs
- 1 3/4 cup all-purpose flour
- 1/4 teaspoon salt
- 1 teaspoon baking powder
- 1/2 cup dried cranberries
- 1 1/2 cup pistachio nuts

Direction

1. Prep oven to 150 ° C

2. Combine the oil and sugar in a large bowl until a homogeneous mixture is obtained. Stir in the vanilla and almond extract and add the eggs. Combine flour, salt, and baking powder; gradually add to the egg mixture — mix cranberries and nuts by hand.

3. Divide the dough in half — form two 12 x 2-inch logs on a parchment baking sheet. The dough can be sticky, wet hands with cold water to make it easier to handle the dough.

4. Bake in the preheated oven for 35 minutes or until the blocks are golden brown. Pullout from the oven and let cool for 10 minutes. Reduce oven heat to 275 degrees F (135 degrees C).

5. Cut diagonally into 3/4-inch-thick slices. Place on the sides on the baking sheet covered with parchment — Bake for about 8 to 10 minutes

Nutrition:

92 calories

4.3g fat

2.1g protein

Cream Puff Dessert

Preparation time: 20 minutes

Cooking Time: 36 minutes

Servings: 12

Ingredients

Puff

- 1 cup water
- 1/2 cup butter
- 1 cup all-purpose flour
- 4 eggs

Filling

- 1 (8-oz) package cream cheese, softened
- 3 1/2 cups cold milk
- 2 (4-oz) packages instant chocolate pudding mix

Topping

- 1 (8-oz) package frozen whipped cream topping, thawed

- 1/4 cup topping with milk chocolate flavor
- 1/4 cup caramel filling
- 1/3 cup almond flakes

Direction:

1. Set oven to 200 degrees C (400 degrees F). Grease a 9 x 13-inch baking dish.
2. Melt the butter in the water in a medium-sized pan over medium heat. Pour the flour in one go and mix vigorously until the mixture forms a ball. Remove from heat and let stand for 5 minutes. Beat the eggs one by one until they are smooth and shiny. Spread in the prepared pan.
3. Bake in the preheated oven for 30 to 35 minutes, until puffed and browned. Cool completely on a rack.
4. While the puff pastry cools, mix the cream cheese mixture, the milk, and the pudding. Spread over the cooled puff pastry. Cool for 20 minutes.
5. Spread whipped cream on cooled topping and sprinkle with chocolate and caramel sauce. Sprinkle with almonds. Freeze 1 hour before serving.

Nutrition:

355 calories

22.3g fat

8.7g protein

Fresh Peach Dessert

Preparation time: 30 minutes

Cooking Time: 27 minutes

Servings: 15

Ingredients

- 16 whole graham crackers, crushed

- 3/4 cup melted butter

- 1/2 cup white sugar

- 4 1/2 cups of miniature marshmallows

- 1/4 cup of milk

- 1 pint of heavy cream

- 1/3 cup of white sugar

- 6 large fresh peaches - peeled, seeded and sliced

Direction:

1. In a bowl, mix the crumbs from the graham cracker, melted butter, and 1/2 cup of sugar. Mix until a homogeneous mixture is obtained, save 1/4 cup of the mixture for filling. Squeeze the rest of the mixture into the bottom of a 9 x 13-inch baking dish.

2. Heat marshmallows and milk in a large pan over low heat and stir until marshmallows are completely melted. Remove from heat and let cool.

3. Beat the cream in a large bowl until soft peaks occur. Beat 1/3 cup of sugar until the cream forms firm spikes. Add the whipped cream to the cooled marshmallow mixture.

4. Divide half of the cream mixture over the crust, place the peaches over the cream and divide the rest of the cream mixture over the peaches. Sprinkle the crumb mixture on the cream. Cool until ready to serve.

Nutrition:

366 calories

22.5g fat

1.9g protein

Blueberry Dessert

Preparation time: 30 minutes

Cooking Time: 20 minutes

Servings: 28

Ingredients

- 1/2 cup butter
- 2 cups white sugar
- 36 graham crackers, crushed
- 4 eggs
- 2 packets of cream cheese, softened
- 1 teaspoon vanilla extract
- 2 cans of blueberry pie filling
- 1 package (16-oz) frozen whipped cream, thawed

Direction:

1. Cook butter and sprinkle 1 cup of sugar and graham crackers. Squeeze this mixture into a 9x13 dish.
2. Beat the eggs. Gradually beat the cream cheese, sugar, and vanilla in the eggs.
3. Pour the mixture of eggs and cream cheese over the graham cracker crust. Bake for 15 to 20 minutes at 165 ° C (325 ° F). Cool.
4. Pour the blueberry pie filling on top of the baked dessert. Spread non-dairy whipped topping on fruit. Cool until ready to serve.

Nutrition:

354 calories

15.4g fat

3.8g protein

Dessert Recipes

CPSIA information can be obtained
at www.ICGtesting.com
Printed in the USA
BVHW011039160621
609724BV00003B/346